American Society for Training & Dev

CREATING TRAINING COURSES

(WHEN YOU'RE *NOT* A TRAINER)

QUICK COURSE DESIGN, DEVELOPMENT, AND DELIVERY FOR SUBJECT MATTER EXPERTS, MANAGERS, AND OTHER NONTRAINERS

Donald V. McCain

ASTD

Ordering Information: Books published by the American Society for Training
& Development can be ordered by calling 800.628.2783 or 703.683.8100.

Library of Congress Catalog Card Number: 99-72433
ISBN: 1-56286-114-X

TABLE OF CONTENTS

Page

Preface v
1 Introduction and Purpose Statement 1
    Introduction 1
    Purpose Statement 1
    Objectives 2
    Instructions for Using this Guide 2
2 Principles of Adult Learning 5
3 Design, Development, and Delivery Processes 7
    Design, Development, and Delivery Table 8
    Phase I: Design Checklist 9
    Phase I: Design 9
        Align With Needs Analysis 10
        Consider Cultural Adaptability 10
        Determine Class: Audience Profile, Mix, and Size 11
        Develop Course Overview, Theme, and Goals 12
        Identify Instructional Strategies 14
        Identify SMEs and Customers for Design Review 15
        Determine Prerequisites 16
        Consider Media....................................17
        Consider Evaluation................................18
        Facilitator Evaluation and Content Relevance 20
    Phase II: Development Checklist 25
    Phase II: Development 26
        Establish Learning Objectives.......................26
        Develop Content and Write Material...................30
        Develop the Instructor/Facilitator Guide 35
        Develop/Secure Participant Materials 37
        Develop Evaluation Instruments 37

Conduct a Pilot Course 37
Phase III: Delivery Checklist 38
Phase III: Delivery 38
    Select Qualified Instructor/Facilitator.....................38
    Conduct Train-the-Trainer 39
    Roll Out Course 40
    Decision Criteria for Selecting Facilitators 40
4 Facilitation Skills 43
    Determine the Role of the Instructor/Facilitator 43
    Establish a Learning Climate 44
    Handle Resistance 44
    Develop Facilitation Skills 45
    Facilitate Instructional Strategies/Learning Activities 49
    Facilitation/Presentation Skills Checklist 52
    Media Decision Table 53
    Hints for Presentations 55
    Hints for Using Visual Aids 55
5 Concluding Remarks 59
Appendices
    Appendix A: Example for Design, Development, and
    Delivery of a Learning Experience 61
    Appendix B: Checklist for Design, Development, and
    Delivery of a Learning Experience 73
    Appendix C: Job Aid for Design, Development, and
    Delivery of a Learning Experience 77
Glossary of Terms 87
Bibliography 91
About the Author 95

PREFACE

As organizations continue to downsize, managers are being asked to accept more responsibility for training their employees. Managers are calling on subject matter experts (SMEs) to share their expertise by providing training for others in their organization. An SME is defined by content knowledge rather than organizational position. Therefore, an SME could be a professional, a manager, or a senior executive with recognized expertise in a particular field. An SME is seen as credible within the organization. This guide provides assistance to SMEs who must now provide such training. *Creating Training Courses (When You're Not a Trainer)* provides a complete description, guide, and supporting job aids for the design, development, and delivery of short classroom courses.

This guide is in the nature of a workbook and procedures manual. Its basic purpose is to guide the SME through the entire design, development, and delivery process and provide continued support in the form of checklists and a job aid. While this guide presents the major steps in the process, it does not adhere strictly to any particular model. This is not a mechanical process, but one that involves thought and creativity. Using this guide, you will develop high-quality programs that enable you to share your expertise while increasing your organization's intellectual capital. For planning purposes, you should consider a design and development ratio of at least 30:1. This means that for every hour of delivery, you should plan on spending 30 hours in design and development.

This publication is dedicated to my wife, Kathy, in recognition of her continued devotion to and support of me and my work. I also want to thank the following for their contribution to *Creating Training Courses (When You're Not a Trainer)*: Stephanie Aichele; Bill Hollaway, NiS Inc.; Jane Dowden; Deborah Tobey, DDT Associates.

1 INTRODUCTION AND PURPOSE STATEMENT

Introduction

Welcome to *Creating Training Courses (When You're Not a Trainer)*. You have been identified as a subject matter expert (SME) within your organization. As such, you have been asked to share your expertise within the organization. The intent of this guide is to identify the many considerations that you must address as you design, develop, and deliver a short training course. Some questions come to mind:

- How will you go about this?
- Do you list things you want to tell your audience?
- What if the audience already knows some of the content?
- How will you know how much the audience already knows about the content?
- If participants can say it, can they put it into practice?
- Can you help participants improve the way they perform?
- How will you arrange to help performance improve?
- How will you know if you have helped your audience?

Purpose Statement

The purpose of *Creating Training Courses (When You're Not a Trainer)* is to assist you in the design, development, and delivery of short classroom-based courses for your organization. This guide will provide you with an opportunity to apply design and development concepts to a course you are to develop. This is an abridged guide to the design, development, and delivery processes and is not intended to provide an in-depth analysis of each process.

Objectives

At the conclusion of this guide, you will be able to

- identify concepts that apply to adult learning
- differentiate between concepts of design and development
- design a short course or workshop
- use effective presentation techniques in the delivery of courses. This guide provides direction for you in
- developing content and materials to meet your internal customers' needs
- organizing and expanding the material you want to use
- conveying this material effectively to your customers and co-workers
- evaluating the learning that has taken place.

Instructions for Using this Guide

This guide contains the following sections: (1) Introduction; (2) Principles of Adult Learning; (3) Design, Development, and Delivery Processes; (4) Facilitation Skills; (5) Concluding Remarks; and (6) Appendices. At the beginning of each phase in the Design, Development, and Delivery Processes section is a checklist of the steps required to implement that process. Check the appropriate box if (1) you are already skilled in that area or (2) you have completed the section. Embedded within each of the processes presented is the opportunity for you to apply that concept to a course you may be currently developing. This allows you to use this guide as a working document. The Facilitation Skills section provides you with several aspects of facilitation, a skills checklist, and media suggestions. The Appendices offer examples and various job aids for course design, development, and delivery and can be used as a baseline for future activity.

2 PRINCIPLES OF ADULT LEARNING

What mental image do you have when someone mentions teacher, instructor, or classroom? Chances are you picture someone standing in front of a class lecturing students, who sit, take notes, and raise their hands to ask questions.

Now shift mental gears. Picture yourself in a business situation where you are enjoying learning something new. This picture is probably different from the previous one, and from it you can discern the qualities that you already realize are important about relating to adults in a training environment.

The following model or acronym helps summarize some of these aspects of adult learning:

Learner Directed

If learners understand *why* they need the information and skills you can give them, the lesson will be easier for them to learn.

Experiential

Adults who are in a learning environment gain more from experiencing the concepts being taught than they do from just a lecture or presentation. They want active involvement and relevance to their job and organization.

A ble to be Evaluated

When you begin to teach a concept, define it. Specify as clearly as possible the result that you want from the learners. Identify what knowledge, skill, or attitude change will take place.

R esidual

Adults learn more effectively if they build on known information, facts, or experiences rather than independent, arbitrary facts. Base the information you give them on their experience and knowledge and lead them into greater depth of that knowledge. Encourage participation. This gives participants a stronger appreciation of learning and also helps others benefit from their experiences.

N umerous Instructional Methods

Some people learn better from verbal instructions; others, from written instructions. Some people learn better from example, while others are visually oriented. Still others learn by trial and error. Remember, adults prefer to use their own experiences in the learning process. There is definitely an advantage in class discussions as opposed to lectures, since adults in the group bring a wide variety of work and life experience with them. Therefore, you want to facilitate discussions to draw out their expertise (see the Residual section above). Plan to incorporate these various methods in your presentations. You reach a wider audience with the variety, provide valuable reinforcement for everyone, and make the learning experience more interesting.

3 DESIGN, DEVELOPMENT, AND DELIVERY PROCESSES

At the heart of any training course are design and development of the content, and instructional strategies. The execution of these is the delivery.

The design lays the foundation of what is to come and is critical to the success of the course. Assess the needs of your particular audience; then make initial plans for the course theme, goals, and objectives. Then plan instructional or learning strategies; method of delivery; choice of media; and the evaluating format.

The development phase adds the detail to the design. This is where specific objectives are written and all of the course substance and instructional strategies are fully developed. Here you will also develop the media, participant materials, and all materials necessary to support the delivery of the course.

How do you know if you are on target with your course design? By seeking input from your internal stakeholder(s) and some future participants. This is formally done through content review and a pilot of the program.

Delivery is where it all comes together. Select the right person to be the facilitator and then train that person to deliver the content and implement the instructional strategies.

Design, Development, and Delivery Table

The following table graphically depicts the program phases addressed above.

DESIGN, DEVELOPMENT, AND DELIVERY

Phase I: Design	*Phase II: Development*	*Phase III: Delivery*
Align with needs analysis	Reference needs assessment	Determine facilitator require-ments
Consider cultural adaptability	Establish learning objectives	Select qualified instructor/facili-tator
Determine class: audience pro-file, mix, and size	Develop content and write material	Conduct train-the-trainer
Develop course overview, theme, and goals	Conduct content review	Roll out course
Identify instructional strategies	Determine and develop instruc-tional strategies	Evaluate
Identify SMEs and customers for design review	Develop/secure media	
Determine prerequisites	Develop the instructor/facilita-tor guide	
Identify preferred delivery mechanism	Develop/secure participant materials	
Consider media	Develop evaluation instru-ments	
Consider evaluation	Conduct a pilot course	

Phase I: Design Checklist

Check the appropriate box (1) if you are already skilled in that area or (2) upon completing the section.

- ☐ Secure needs analysis data
- ☐ Consider cultural adaptability
- ☐ Identify target audience
    - ☐ Understand audience profile
    - ☐ Determine class mix
    - ☐ Determine class size
- ☐ Align course content to needs analysis
- ☐ Develop course theme
- ☐ Develop course goals
- ☐ Develop high-level outline
- ☐ Consider flow/format for the modules
- ☐ Identify initial instructional strategies
- ☐ Identify SMEs and customers for design review
- ☐ Determine prerequisites
- ☐ Identify preferred delivery mechanism
- ☐ Consider media
- ☐ Consider evaluation

Phase I: Design

The design phase is critical to the success of course development. It forms the basis for the inclusion or exclusion of content, instructional strategies, and media. Time spent in the design stage is time well spent.

Align With Needs Analysis

What do the participants need to know or do?

Needs analysis is the process of determining if there is a need to improve performance and, if so, in what area and to what extent. The *need* is the gap between desired and actual performance. As a subject matter expert (SME) about to design and develop a course, the need or needs should have already been identified.

In the space below, state the identified needs for the course you are designing. (See page 61 for an example.)

_____

_____

_____

_____

Consider Cultural Adaptability

What are the differences among your participants?

This simply translates to knowing your audience. Because many organizations are international, you have probably had experience in and with classes where cultural issues, characteristics, and protocol have been incorporated into the learning experience. Making cultural accommodations results in a more effective learning experience for all involved.

The following are some hints for cultural adaptability:

■ Provide many handouts, deep in content.
■ Make sure that the media has enough text to put the content in context.
■ Be sensitive to in-country values and norms.
■ Use stories and examples that relate to the culture.

- Pilot all materials and activities with the target audience.
- Translate material into the country language where possible.
- Use a translator if appropriate.
- Align instructional strategies with country norms.
- Avoid inappropriate pictures and words.
- Provide detailed instructions for activities.
- Use plenty of pictures, visual aids, and demonstrations.

Determine Class: Audience Profile, Mix, and Size

Who are your participants?

Based on the needs analysis, you have determined a target audience for the course content. The audience profile refers to the information you have about those being trained. Members of your training or human resource department can assist in securing information about your audience. They will consult with you to provide you with needed information on your participants. You may want information regarding a business function; pay grades, the organization, and industry experience; gender; educational background; learning attitudes; job environment; and skills and experiences.

A mix by culture would have been considered above. The mix by gender, age, or both might determine the effectiveness of the analogies you use in your presentation. A mix of corporate experience (job, function, and pay grade) may affect the business acumen of the collective group. Consider how culture, gender, age, and corporate characteristics may affect your course content or method and your style of communicating.

Just as a mix of class members helps to ensure interaction, you also want to consider the mix of an individual team. Do you want to put a manager and a direct report on the same team? What is the potential impact on openness, creativity, and risk taking?

The size of the group also affects the development and use of instructional strategies. A very small group—say, six to eight—might not lend itself to complicated case studies and feedback using multiple teams.

In the space on the next page, profile your audience. (See page 61 for an example.)

_____

_____

_____

_____

Develop Course Overview, Theme, and Goals

What is the course content, and what do I want to accomplish?

At this point, you have decided you want to design a course for adult learners, and you have some ideas about what is of interest to them. Now you have to decide what you want the course to include and accomplish. You have been selected as an SME.

In the space below, briefly state the aspects of your area of expertise that you want to share with your audience, and describe the results you would like for your audience to gain from your information. (See page 62 for an example.)

Area of expertise

_____

_____

_____

_____

_____

Results

_____

_____

_____

_____

_____

Based on the needs analysis, write a theme statement and goals for the course. The theme is usually one sentence that captures the essence of what the learning experience will accomplish. For example, the theme for a sales management course might be Leading the Sales Team of the Future While Creating a Competitive Advantage and High Customer Satisfaction. The theme captures the ongoing change that is to take place, beginning with the learning experience and continuing back on the job. The goals are statements of what you want the course to accomplish in light of the needs of the audience. The module learning objectives (to be developed later) will then support the course goals. The theme and course goals will become threads connecting the content.

In the space below, write your course theme and goals. (See pages 62–63 for an example.)

Theme

_____

_____

_____

_____

Goals

_____

_____

_____

Next, develop a high-level outline to describe content areas and the flow of information. The content outline will have major headings supported by **at least** one level of detail. It can follow an outline format. By adding module objectives to major outline content areas, you are developing the macro design. Then, for each content area, have a consistent format for development. A suggested format is warm-up, content presentation, application, reinforcement. The warm-up is some form of activity or discussion that introduces the upcoming content and links it to the previous discussion. The content is the material developed that presents the knowledge, skill, or attitude change desired. Application refers to using the content in a simulated or real situation and linking the content to the job. This can be accomplished through your instructional strategies, discussed next. Reinforcement is the summary or repetition of the content, the application of that content, or both. This basic flow can then be repeated for each module that has significantly different content.

Identify Instructional Strategies

How do I want to present the information and involve the participants?

The term instructional strategies describes the methodology used to help participants become involved and learn. Examples include role plays, case studies, facilitated discussions, small team problem solving or exercises, games, simulations, peer teaching, and so forth. The instructional strategies chosen should align with the content being presented and enhance the learning process. Use these strategies to reinforce content and provide application to a real job situation.

In the space below, write your content outline and initial

instructional strategies. Use additional paper as needed. (See page 63 for an example.)

Content Outline	Instructional Strategies
_____	_____
_____	_____
_____	_____
_____	_____
_____	_____
_____	_____
_____	_____
_____	_____
_____	_____
_____	_____

Identify SMEs and Customers for Design Review

Who needs to review the design?

Include other SMEs and your customers (course participants and stakeholders) to validate the direction of the course theme, goals, and macro design. Their involvement also begins the process of buy-in and ownership.

In the space below, indicate the people who need to review the design. (See page 64 for an example.)

_____

_____

_____

Determine Prerequisites

What knowledge, skill, or experience should participants have prior to taking this course?

Make an initial identification of any precourse requirements that are needed for participants to be ready for the course. This may include prereads that you provide, other courses, job experiences, or college or technical education. If participants do not have the prerequisites, should they attend the course?

In the space below, identify prerequisites for the course you are designing. (See page 64 for an example.)

_____

_____

_____

Identify Preferred Delivery Mechanism

What medium do I use to deliver the content?

The following should be considered in determining your delivery mechanism:

- the topic
- acceptability to the audience
- audience size and geographic dispersion
- resources (dollars and time).

Some subjects lend themselves to computer-based training (CBT); others require group interaction. Choices include CBT, classroom, self-paced study, distance learning, job rotation, and coaching or mentoring. Consult your training department or contact a professional trainer for recommendations on delivery. You have the option of using multiple delivery methods. For example, you may use CBT for prework to support a classroom delivery.

In the space below, indicate the delivery mechanism or mechanisms for the course you are designing. (See page 64 for an example.)

_____

_____

_____

Consider Media

What media do I want to use?

Media are helpful in enhancing the learning process. A variety of well-chosen media holds participants' attention and aids in communication. At this stage in the design process, begin considering a choice of media to help drive content and learning. Some forms of media include flip charts, PowerPoint, whiteboard, overheads, videos, 35 mm slides, development and use of models, and computer projection. Some factors in deciding include the following:

- equipment available in the training room
- availability of technical support
- number of deliveries
- central delivery versus multiple locations
- time and budget for production
- audience preferences
- your skill level
- setup of the training facility or room.

Your training department or a training professional can help you to determine media.

In the space below, indicate your initial media for the course you are designing. (See page 64 for an example.)

_____

_____

_____

Consider Evaluation

Was the course successful?

The initial reaction of the participants is one form of evaluation. This is called level 1 evaluation. Through a structured form, you can secure input regarding such things as the following:

■ the extent to which the objectives were met
■ the skills and knowledge of the facilitator
■ the quality and effectiveness of participant materials and media
■ relevance to the job
■ effectiveness of the instructional strategies.

(See pages 20–24 of this chapter for an example of this form of evaluation.)

A second concern is whether learning took place. This is level 2 evaluation and can be accomplished through pre- and posttesting for knowledge gained (using objective tests, such as true-or-false, matching, fill-in-the-blank, and so forth); through evaluating your application, instructional strategies, and exercises; or both. To assess the application of your content, checklists would need to be developed to evaluate the degree to which the participants can apply the new knowledge or skill. The checklists are developed in conjunction with selected instructional strategies. Usually, the checklists require a yes-or-no or scaled responses, such as 1-4, 1-5, or 1-10. You could give a skill test for mastery. For example, if you are teaching keyboarding, test for speed and accuracy. In some cases, you have organizational standards or specifications (for production jobs) that become your pass-or-fail score.

Third, is the learning being used on the job, and if so, to what extent? This is level 3 evaluation. If the new skills are not being used, the evaluation should address the reasons for lack of transfer. It could be that the environment does not support the new skills. This could be due to lack of management support, peer pressure, or a reward system that does not reward the use of the new skills. The evaluation should identify the inhibitors to successful transfer. If transfer is taking place, the evaluation should also identify those enablers that support the transfer of the skill training. This form of evaluation can be conducted through (1) before-and-after comparisons; (2) observations, supported by behavioral checklists or feedback from the participant's manager, direct reports, and peers; (3) statistical comparisons of before-and-after training performance; and (4) "moments of truth" or critical incidents that provide an opportunity for a person to demonstrate the new skill or behavior.

Last, what is the impact of the training on the organization? This form of evaluation, called level 4 evaluation, relates the results of the program to organizational improvement. Results that can be examined include cost savings, improved productivity, changes in quality, return on investment (ROI), increased revenue, improved customer satisfaction, increased market share, reduced turnover, reduction in scrap or defects, fewer grievances, and so forth. This involves collecting data before (for the baseline) and after the program and analyzing the improvement. The most difficult part of this evaluation is separating the variables to identify the role training played in the business change.

The development of an evaluation process and supporting instruments is a specialized skill that resides in your training department. Contact your training department or a training professional for assistance in implementing your evaluation requirements. Some sources for evaluation include the following:

Broad, Mary and John Newstrom. *Transfer of Training*. New York: Addison-Wesley Publishing Company, 1992.

Dixon, Nancy. *Evaluation: A Tool for Improving HRD Quality*. San Diego: University Associates Inc., 1990.

Kirkpatrick, Donald. *Evaluating Training Programs: The Four Levels*. San Francisco: Berrett-Koehler Publishers, 1994.

Phillips, Jack. *Handbook of Training Evaluation and Measurement Methods*. Houston: Gulf Publishing Company, 1991.

Phillips, Jack. "ROI: The Search for Best Practices." *Training & Development*, volume 50, number 2, February 1996.

Phillips, Jack. "Was it the Training?" *Training & Development*, volume 50, number 3, March 1996.

Phillips, Jack. "How Much is the Training Worth? *Training & Development*, volume 50, number 4, April 1996.

Robinson, Dana Gaines and Jim Robinson. "Training for Impact." *Training & Development Journal*, volume 43, number 8, August 1989.

Robinson, Dana Gaines and Jim Robinson. *Training for Impact: How to Link Training to Business Needs and Measure the Results*. San Francisco: Jossey-Bass Publishers, 1989.

Facilitator Evaluation and Content Relevance

I. Course Information

Course Title: _____

Date(s): _____

Instructor/Facilitator: _____

Location: _____

Job Function/Business Unit: _____

Job Title: _____

The statements below concern specific aspects of the course. Please indicate to what extent you agree with each statement by circling the appropriate number. Please use the following scale:

Not Applicable=N/A   Strongly Disagree=1   Disagree=2
Agree=3   Strongly Agree=4

II. Course Content

1. Objectives were clearly explained   N/A 1   2   3   4
2. Participant ideas were relevant to content and incorporated in the discussion   N/A 1   2   3   4
3. Objectives stated were met (write in objectives)
   - ■   N/A 1   2   3   4
   - ■   N/A 1   2   3   4
   - ■   N/A 1   2   3   4
   - ■   N/A 1   2   3   4
   - ■   N/A 1   2   3   4
   - ■   N/A 1   2   3   4
   - ■   N/A 1   2   3   4
   - ■   N/A 1   2   3   4
4. Content is relevant to my function (if disagree, please explain)   N/A 1   2   3   4

Comments:

_____
_____
_____
_____
_____

III. Course Methodology

The following activities/materials helped me understand the content and achieve the objectives:

5. Preread	N/A	1	2	3	4
6. Case study	N/A	1	2	3	4
7. Audio/Visual (Flip charts, videos, tapes, etc.)	N/A	1	2	3	4
8. Exercises and/or Activities	N/A	1	2	3	4
9. Written Assignments	N/A	1	2	3	4
10. Facilitated Discussions	N/A	1	2	3	4
11. Participant Guide	N/A	1	2	3	4
12.	N/A	1	2	3	4
13.	N/A	1	2	3	4
14.	N/A	1	2	3	4

Comments:

_____

_____

_____

IV. Instructor/Facilitator

15. Promoted an environment of learning	N/A	1	2	3	4
16. Presented clearly to assist my understanding	N/A	1	2	3	4
17. Appeared knowledgeable about the subject matter	N/A	1	2	3	4
18. Provided feedback effectively to participants	N/A	1	2	3	4
19. Presented content in an appropriate sequence	N/A	1	2	3	4

20. Promoted participant discussion and involvement	N/A	1	2	3	4
21. Kept the discussion on topic and activities on track	N/A	1	2	3	4
22. Demonstrated an understanding of the organization	N/A	1	2	3	4
23. Demonstrated and referenced personal experience	N/A	1	2	3	4
24.	N/A	1	2	3	4
25.	N/A	1	2	3	4
26.	N/A	1	2	3	4

Comments:

_____

_____

_____

V. Environment and Administrative Support

27. Registration process was effective	N/A	1	2	3	4
28. Course materials were received in a timely manner	N/A	1	2	3	4
29. Training room was appropriate in size and arrangement	N/A	1	2	3	4
30. Training room was clean, well lit, and ventilated	N/A	1	2	3	4
31. Meals and breaks were on time and appetizing	N/A	1	2	3	4
32. Promotional material was accurate and informative	N/A	1	2	3	4
33.	N/A	1	2	3	4
34.	N/A	1	2	3	4

Comments:

_____

_____

_____

VI. Summary

	Poor	Fair	Good	Excellent
35. Overall rating for the course	1	2	3	4

36. Would you recommend the course
to your peers?   ☐ Yes   ☐ No

Comments:

_____

_____

_____

Please share any information you believe would help us to improve this course:

_____

_____

_____

Briefly describe any training areas you would like addressed in the next 18 months:

_____

_____

_____

Thank you for taking the time to share your comments and your reactions to this experience!

Phase II: Development Checklist

Check the appropriate box (1) if you are already skilled in that area or (2) upon completing the section.

- ☐ Establish learning objectives
  - ☐ Determine that they are measurable
  - ☐ Determine that they contain the performance, conditions, and criteria components
- ☐ Develop content and write materials
- ☐ Determine that content links to and supports learning objectives
  - ☐ Conduct content review
  - ☐ Invite appropriate participants
  - ☐ Make revisions
  - ☐ Develop instructional strategies
  - ☐ Determine that instructional strategies support the content and learning objectives
  - ☐ Develop/secure the media
  - ☐ Determine that the media supports the content and enhances learning
- ☐ Determine classroom layout to support the design and instructional strategies
- ☐ Develop instructor/facilitator guide
- ☐ Develop/secure participant materials
  - ☐ Develop participant manual
  - ☐ Develop/secure preread materials
  - ☐ Develop instruments for action planning
  - ☐ Develop required instruction pages and worksheets
- ☐ Develop evaluation instruments
- ☐ Conduct a course pilot
  - ☐ Invite appropriate participants
  - ☐ Make revisions

Phase II: Development

Reference the needs analysis and audience profile information provided by the training department.

Establish Learning Objectives

What should the participants be able to do?

The learning objectives:

- Define the output of the design and development process in terms of what the participant should be able to know, do, or both.
- Set boundaries to help determine what content should be included and, just as important, what content should not be included.

Realistically, learning objectives usually state what the participants will understand or be able to apply. For the actual course, your learning objectives should include three components: performance, conditions, and criteria.

Performance: *What will the learner will be able to do as a result of the training?*

These skills should be measurable. Consider the following (see page 28 for additional verbs):

Measurable	*Indefinite*
Calculate	Analyze
Demonstrate/apply	Appreciate
Identify	Consider
List	Understand

Using measurable statements does *not* disregard the fact that you want employees to analyze, appreciate, consider, and understand. Those aspects are important even if they do not constitute measurable objectives.

Conditions: *What are the limitations or constraints under which performance is expected to take place?*

The learner cannot calculate, demonstrate/apply, and so forth (measurable statements) without using certain tools. A carpenter cannot effectively demonstrate hammering a nail into a piece of wood if he or she doesn't have the hammer, nail, and wood. Ideally, you want the learner to apply the knowledge using certain tools, equipment, processes, procedures, and so forth. Therefore, the objectives should specify what the learner will be provided with in order to perform the skill or demonstrate the knowledge. Some examples include computer hardware, software programs, manuals, or job aids.

VERBS

Knowledge	*Skill/application*
Classify	Align
Describe	Arrange
Define	Assemble
Discuss	Budget
Explain	Build
Interpret	Classify
Label	Conduct
Name	Construct
Recognize	Design
Select	Develop
Write	Draw
	Erect
	Evaluate
	Facilitate
	Forecast
	Implement
	Inspect
	Install
	Instruct
	Justify
	Negotiate
	Organize
	Perform
	Plan
	Recommend
	Repair
	Sort
	Synthesize
	Test
	Translate

Criteria: *What is acceptable performance?*

The criteria in the objectives will stipulate how well the learners can perform the tasks or how they can measure improvement over previous behavior. To continue with the example above, if the carpenter doesn't get the nail straight into the wood, the finished product will lack value. Therefore, the wording of the objectives will also include a level of performance desired. These become statements of quality, time, completeness, and so forth.

The first module would also include participant introduction, course agenda, participant expectations, programs norms or standard operating procedures, facilitator introduction, theme and goals, and so forth. In the space below, write your learning objectives to meet the criteria for each module or unit you defined in your content outline. Use additional paper if required. (See page 65 for an example.)

Module 1

_____

_____

_____

Module 2

_____

_____

_____

Module 3

_____

_____

_____

Module 4

Develop Content and Write Material

What content do I want to present?

Develop/write the content

You are now ready to develop and actually write the content for the course. Because you are an SME, you may not need to do a great deal of research on the actual topic. While some prefer to develop full scripts, brief statements supported with bullet points will generally provide the necessary content for a facilitator who is also an SME. Check recent publications for additional explanations and the most current material. You may want to provide your participants with a bibliography.

The content can be divided into three areas: the introduction, the body—including the presentation of the underlying theory and skill development—and the summary. This format can be used for an entire course or for lessons or modules within a course.

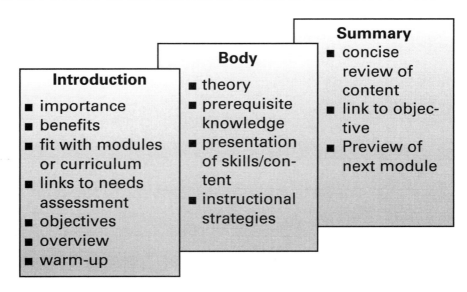

Introduction
- importance
- benefits
- fit with modules or curriculum
- links to needs assessment
- objectives
- overview
- warm-up

Body
- theory
- prerequisite knowledge
- presentation of skills/content
- instructional strategies

Summary
- concise review of content
- link to objective
- Preview of next module

Introduction: This section should include a statement of the benefits and importance of the course to the participants, how the lesson or module fits into the course or how the course fits into the curriculum (if appropriate), the link to the needs assessment, the learning objectives, and an outline or overview of the material to be presented, including the course theme and goals. You also include the warm-up in the introduction to introduce the content of that module. Warm-up should also be used to begin the course to create an open and comfortable learning environment that fosters participation.

Body: theory and skill development: This section presents the relevant theory underlying the skills to be developed. It includes a review of the prerequisite knowledge that a person needs in order to understand and perform the skills to be taught. The skill development includes the presentation and modeling of the particular skill to be taught. In this section, include the instructional strategies to apply the course content.

Summary: This section is a concise presentation of the key information, linking that information back to the learning objectives and benefits. If appropriate, provide a preview to the next lesson or course that this content supports.

In the space below, indicate the course or module benefits to the participants, the link to prior and subsequent modules or courses, and the link to the needs assessment. (See pages 65–68 for an example.)

Benefits:

_____

_____

_____

_____

_____

Link/fit to prior and subsequent modules or courses:

_____

_____

_____

Link to needs assessment:

_____

_____

_____

Link to learning objectives

First, write what you want to say. *Be sure that the content directly relates to the learning objectives.* The objectives and content should be consistent with the course theme and goal or goals. Use the learning objectives as a constant check for what information to include and exclude. The warm-up exercise introduces the content to follow.

In the space below, describe your warm-up exercise. (See pages 65–66 for an example.)

_____

_____

_____

Conduct content review

The content review gives you the opportunity to get input and buy-in on the content *only*. The intent is for validation and support. In this meeting, you do not present the instructional strategies or media ideas. The developer wants input as to the completeness of the information, the presence of extraneous material, the logic of the flow, the linkages between sections of material, the consistency with learning objectives, and the application to the learner's job.

The participants in the content review should include the SMEs and customers indicated earlier and a representative sample of the target audience. Usually, eight to 12 participants should provide the necessary input.

In the space below, indicate whom you will invite to the content review. Some of these participants include those who participated in the design review. (See page 69 for an example.)

_____

_____

_____

Your training department or a training professional will provide necessary support regarding the format and suggestions for the content review. Consider the responses from the content review, and incorporate the suggestions you believe are appropriate. Remember, you are the SME. The final decisions belong to you. Also remember that the participants in the content review will be looking to see if their suggestions were incorporated into the final course.

Determine and develop instructional strategies

Next, fully develop the instructional strategies with complete directions you considered in the design stage on page 9. (Use additional paper for this work.) The instructional strategies are the learning activities that involve the participants in the content and provide application of the content. Materials can be designed for individuals, small teams or subgroups, or the entire group. The key is to match the instructional strategy to the content and participants' preferences. You also want the instructional strategies to simulate reality as closely as possible. This aids with job transfer and holds the participants' interest.

Some examples of instructional strategies include the following:

■ Ask predetermined questions to build discussion.

■ Ask large group questions and chart the answers or brainstorm.

■ Ask the large group a series of questions and have groups of two or three develop a response to one or more of the questions. The groups then report back, and other groups can add to or modify the responses.

■ Conduct role plays.

■ Use case studies, purchased or developed.

■ Use computer-based simulations or exercises.

■ Present live issues and have teams work on a solution based on the course content and their experience. The teams present their solutions to a panel or the other participants for dialogue.

■ You can also be more creative. For example, have participants write songs, poems, or plays that reflect the course content.

Remember, the instructional strategies that are developed must have the "answers," debrief comments, or both to reinforce the course content.

Develop/secure media

You are now ready to develop or secure the necessary media to support the content and the instructional strategies. Adults learn more easily if there is a mix of methods, such as visual and verbal; you might have flipcharts or overhead transparencies with brief outlines, diagrams, an occasional cartoon that illustrates a point, a short section of a video, or handouts to describe a case study or group discussion. Use a skilled person in media development to produce overheads and flipcharts. This adds an element of quality and professionalism to the course. Your training department or a training professional can help with the media.

Note: It is a good idea to have handouts that duplicate the wording of the prepared overheads and flipcharts you use. This keeps the learners from spending too much time copying and taking notes instead of listening and interacting.

Determine classroom layout

You will need to determine the best room design or setup. This is a design and development issue. If your participants are to be in teams, your room design should reflect this. You may need break-out rooms for some activities. There are multiple room layout options. Your training department or a training professional can help you determine the optimum design for your course. (See page 36 for some recommended layouts.)

Develop the Instructor/Facilitator Guide

How do I develop my teaching notes?

This is the equivalent of a leader's guide, an answer book, and timetable combined. It should be complete enough so that any qualified instructor or facilitator, with little effort, could teach the course. The facilitator's guide should include the following:

- questions to be asked and suggested answers for questions posed
- all instructions for the instructional strategies and debrief comments (your summary comments based on content, the "answers") for those instructional strategies
- a guide listing the main points to teach in each section, what media and activities you plan to use with those points, and the amount of time you will allow for modules, instructional strategies, breaks, and other activities
- a section providing a listing of all handouts, materials and supplies, the seating arrangement, and media.

Your training department or a training professional can assist you by suggesting a particular format to meet your needs.

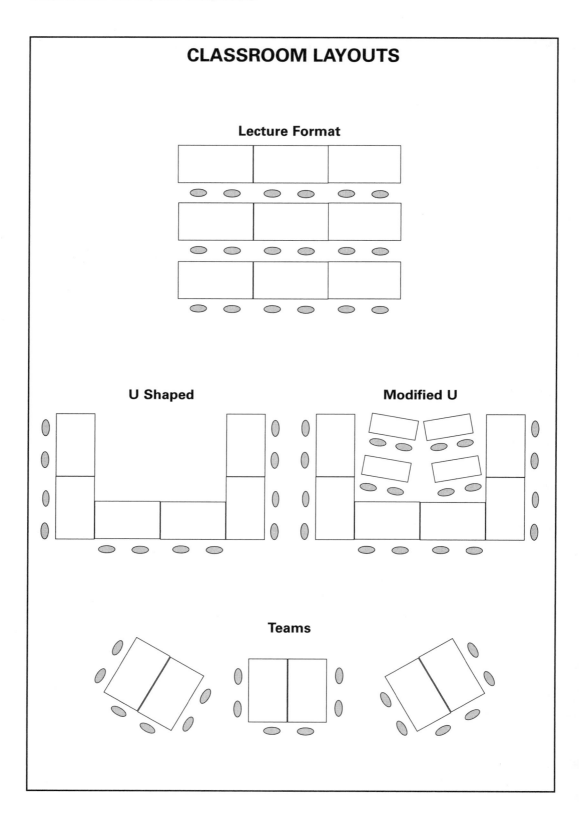

CLASSROOM LAYOUTS

Lecture Format

U Shaped

Modified U

Teams

Develop/Secure Participant Materials

What is included in the participant materials?

The participant materials include any preread materials, instructions and worksheets for instructional strategies, a participant manual, examples, a "strategy booklet" or action-planning document for transfer to the job, and any other materials necessary to support participants' learning.

Develop Evaluation Instruments

What evaluation instruments should I use?

While you considered the evaluation process and instruments in the design stage, you are now ready to develop the actual instruments. The evaluation instruments for the course pilot will be much more extensive than those used for the ongoing delivery. Your training department or a training professional will help you develop an evaluation process and evaluation instruments. These will become the measuring devices for ongoing course management and course value.

Conduct a Pilot Course

How can I test the course before delivery?

At this point, you will teach the course for the first time. In consultation with your training department or a training professional, determine if you want to invite designated individuals from the target audience or have open enrollment for the pilot. Some of the participants should be those who participated in the content review. This will help provide continuity throughout the process.

Based on the evaluation input from the pilot, revise any portions of the course, instructional strategies, media, or participant materials you think should be changed. Once all revisions are made, you are ready for rollout. (Depending on the amount of revision, you may elect to conduct a second pilot.)

Phase III: Delivery Checklist

Check the appropriate box (1) if you are already skilled in that area or (2) upon completing the section.

- [ ] Select qualified instructor/facilitator
    - [ ] Determine that the instructor is knowledgeable of the company, business function/unit, and subject matter
    - [ ] Determine that the instructor is experienced in facilitation
    - [ ] Determine that the instructor is credible with the audience
    - [ ] Determine that the instructor has compatible values
- [ ] Conduct train-the-trainer
    - [ ] Prepare materials
    - [ ] Prepare media
    - [ ] Complete administrative/logistical support
- [ ] Roll out course
    - [ ] Secure support from your training department

Phase III: Delivery

Select Qualified Instructor/Facilitator

Who should deliver the course?

Think back for a minute to some of the introductory remarks about how adults learn. Other adults, just like you, won't respond well to a "canned" lecture or a memorized presentation. Regardless of how scholarly your message is, if it isn't presented well, people won't respond well.

Because of the nature of this assignment, the selection of a qualified instructor is limited to the SMEs or a credible facilitator from an outside vendor. The fact that someone knows the material does not guarantee that he or she can facilitate a learning experience.

Develop criteria to select facilitators. Some dimensions to consider include the following:

■ their knowledge of the content, the organization, and the business function/unit

■ their years of experience in facilitation

■ their references within the organization and other companies

■ their credibility with the target audience

■ their availability on a consistent basis

■ their compatibility of values and style.

The use of a decision matrix can help to identify qualified facilitators.

Decision Criteria for Selecting Facilitators

Following is a decision matrix to assist you in qualifying and selecting facilitators to support your delivery.

Instructions:

1. Add to or modify the existing criteria.
2. Select the criteria to be considered.
3. Weigh each criterion, allocating a total of 100 points among the selected criteria.
4. Rate each potential facilitator against the selected criteria using a 1-5 scale:

   1=poor   2=fair   3=good   4=very good   5=excellent

5. Multiply the weight by the rating to get the total.
6. Add up the total column; select the candidate(s) with the highest score(s).

Criteria	Weight	Rating	Total
■ Management experience			
■ Technical experience within the area			
■ Professional experience within the area			
■ Depth/breadth of experience within the organization			
■ Total years of experience in the area			
■ Total years of experience with the organization			
■ Depth of content knowledge			
■ Bachelor degree within the field			
■ Masters degree within the field			
■ Internal reputation/credibility			
■ Industry recognition			
■ Industry knowledge			
■ Verbal communication skills			
■ Nonverbal communication skills			
■ Listening skills			
■ Professional image (dress, vocabulary)			
■ Need for structure and direction			
■ Facilitation skills			
■			
■			

Total   100

Conduct Train-the-Trainer
How do the instructors/facilitators learn the course?

If the designer or developer is not the facilitator, a train-the-trainer session to train the facilitator or facilitators will be necessary. The training includes all aspects of the course content, instructional strategies, and media to be delivered to the target audience. Allow time for those being trained to practice the delivery of content so you can provide feedback.

An ideal sequence of activities for train-the-trainer is as follows:
1. Trainer is involved in the content review and pilot.
2. Trainer attends the train-the-trainer course.
3. Trainer receives facilitation skills training, if needed.
4. Trainer observes the first delivery.
5. Trainer cofacilitates one or more deliveries.
6. Trainer delivers the content with the SME observing and providing feedback.
7. Trainer continues to deliver the course, using evaluation data as feedback.

Roll Out Course
How do I make the course available to the intended audience?

Work with your training or human resource department for administrative and logistical support. This will include promoting the course and registering participants; scheduling and determining locations for delivery; securing facilities and equipment; setting up the room; and purchasing, duplicating, and shipping materials.

For each delivery, arrive at the location early. The room may not be set up according to your specifications, and participant materials may not be distributed. You will also need to be sure that there are enough markers and flipcharts to support your activities. Do the flipcharts have enough paper? Do the participants have place cards and name tags? Does all of the equipment work? Does the overhead have an extra bulb? How do the learners receive and send messages? Regarding rollout, the devil is in the details. Time is very well spent making sure the incidentals are in order.

4 FACILITATION SKILLS

If you need practice in presentation and facilitation skills, enroll in a class on presentation and facilitation skills. This guide will present some basic facilitation practices and concepts, but it does not afford you the opportunity to practice the skills and receive feedback.

Determine the Role of the Instructor/Facilitator

What is the role of the facilitator?

As an educational facilitator, your approach and everything you say and do should be focused on helping the participants to learn. Your job is to provide an environment whereby interacting with you and other participants will stimulate participants to acquire parts of the skills, knowledge, and attitudes that you possess. Your primary role is to help people learn.

To accomplish this, your job is to enter into a partnership with participants in the learning experience and help them feel comfortable with learning, feel challenged, feel inspired, and become more competent. It is not your job to lecture. Incorporating the adult learning principles presented earlier (page 5) will help ensure a successful experience for you and the participants.

Establish a Learning Climate

How can a facilitator develop a climate for learning?

To establish and maintain a learning climate:

■ Share with participants the session goals and how you plan to achieve them.

■ Describe your role as a presenter and facilitator.

■ Let people know you welcome questions and that you want an interactive session; verbalize it and model it.

■ Demonstrate an open, caring, nonjudgmental attitude.

■ Even though you're an SME, do not create an impression that you know it all.

■ Take the learning process seriously.

Handle Resistance

How can a facilitator handle participants' resistance?

Spotting resistance

Some clues to resistance include the following:

■ continual questioning by those who are trying to make a point rather than gain knowledge

■ participants engaging in numerous side conversations

■ negative or negligent participation in group work

■ a refusal to participate

■ disruptive or inappropriate behavior

■ questions that challenge the relevance of the training or the competence of the facilitator.

Hints for overcoming resistance

■ Look within yourself:

1. Is there anything you are doing or saying that could be seen as controlling?

   2. Do you have a supportive attitude?

   3. Be patient; demonstrate respect for the participants.

■ Consult:

   1. Find out why the participants think they are there.

   2. Find out what would make the training useful.

■ Offer an opportunity for participant reaction:

   1. Find out what is not relevant or important to them.

   2. Provide an opportunity for venting fears, frustrations, anger, and so forth.

   3. Solicit participants' help in determining how the learning could be made more meaningful.

■ Confront directly:

   1. Speak to the disruptive participants at the break and seek their support.

   2. If all else fails and someone persists in interfering with the learning of others, ask the person to leave. Use discretion in deciding what, if anything, to communicate to the person's manager.

Develop Facilitation Skills

How can a facilitator involve participants in the discussions?

Question asking

   Asking questions is a critical facilitator skill. Questions can be closed or open-ended.

   Closed questions generally result in yes-or-no or other one-word answers. They should only be used when you want precise, short answers. Otherwise, they inhibit discussion.

   The open-ended question requires elaboration. For example, "Tell us what you agree or disagree with about that perspective" seeks information. *How*, *what*, and *why* are words that begin open-ended questions.

Asking questions helps you
- provide insights into participants' understanding of the content
- involve participants in a discussion
- model the interaction between the participants and the facilitator, thereby helping to set an open environment for discussion
- get participants' attention and motivate them to listen.

Summarizing

The purpose of summarizing is to
- pull important ideas, facts, information, and learnings together
- establish a basis for further discussion or to make a transition
- review progress
- check for clarity, agreement, or both.

By using summarizing in a conversation, you can encourage people to be more reflective about their positions as they listen for accuracy and emphasis. Summarizing requires you to listen carefully in order to organize and present information systematically. Summarized information ensures that everyone in the discussion is clear about what transpired.

Some starter phrases to help you begin summarizing are as follows:
- There seem to be some key ideas expressed here...
- If I understand you, you feel this way about (describe the situation)...
- I think we agree on this—what we are saying is that we intend to...
- In talking about this issue, we have come up with three main points...

Summarizing gives you the opportunity to check for understanding and agreement. If people do not understand or agree with the content, it is better for you to know during the discussion than to find out later that an instructional objective was not met.

Paraphrasing

Paraphrasing is restating in your own words what the other person has said. This skill strengthens your listening skills and lets the participant know that you are listening and understanding. You can begin paraphrasing by using phrases such as the following:

■ You are saying...

■ In other words...

■ I gather that...

■ If I understand what you are saying...

It is helpful to paraphrase fairly often, so that you develop a habit of doing so. You can even tactfully interrupt to do so, since people generally don't resent interruptions that communicate understanding.

Other facilitation skills

There are other facilitation skills, some verbal, some non-verbal. Examples include the following:

■ nodding one's head

■ picking up on the last word or two of someone else's sentence and using that to reinforce the content or to transition to other content

■ repeating a sentence or part of a sentence

■ asking someone, "Tell us more about that"

■ saying, "That's good. Does anybody else have anything to add?"

■ maintaining eye contact, and an open body position

■ saying, "Uh huh."

Timing and pace: What do I do if I get behind?

Every delivery is different because every audience is different. Some groups are more interactive and ask more questions. Other groups take longer to do the various activities. Yet there is only so much time allotted for the training, and you will need to finish on time. The key is to plan ahead of time what to do if you get behind. Then execute your ideas. Some key actions to take include the following:

1. Identify content that is "must know" versus "nice to know" and "must do" versus "nice to do." Your course learning objectives will provide guidance. Then, if you get behind on your schedule, you can provide the "nice to know" and "nice to do" content by lecture or large group discussion while covering the highlights, or you can abbreviate the activities. This will reduce time.

2. Identify content the learners are most likely familiar with. You can then ask them to review the content briefly in their participant materials. Then ask if there are questions.

3. Alter instructions for activities. For example, the instructions indicate that each group is to give feedback on four questions for a case study. To save time, yet still support the learning, you could have team one respond to question one. Ask other teams if they had anything substantially different. Then team two responds to question two, and other teams respond with the differences, and so on. Another situation could be one in which you want teams to conduct a role play. If the content is somewhat familiar, the facilitator could demonstrate or model the behavior and debrief the learnings. If time allows, a few pairs could then attempt the role play for the entire class, which plays the role of observer.

4. Delete some examples or stories. This will reduce the time spent clarifying points. Do this for content that is somewhat familiar to the learners.

5. Start on time. In many cases, the lost time is due to people not coming back from breaks and lunch on time. This should be a ground rule. If only a few people are present, begin! This will encourage others to be back on time.

6. As an alternative, try to have a working lunch or shorten the time for breaks and lunches. If you do this, be sure the learners perceive value for the time spent.

Facilitate Instructional Strategies/Learning Activities

How does a facilitator go about facilitating instructional strategies and learning activities?

The following is designed to assist you to prepare for and facilitate various instructional strategies or learning activities. The content is organized by instructional strategy and supported by what you can do to prepare for and facilitate each activity.

Lecture: Use to deliver key information when the learners are not familiar with the content.

To Prepare	*To Facilitate*
■ Identify learning points.	■ Keep to your plan.
■ Arrange learning points in sequence.	■ Encourage questions and interaction.
■ Develop discussion questions for each learning point.	■ Know the learning points, but do not memorize a script.
■ Build in transitions between learning points.	■ Cover each learning point.
	■ Lecture no more than 15 to 20 minutes at a time.
	■ Make transition to next content.

Facilitation/guided discussion: Use to deliver information and content when the learners are familiar with the subject.

To Prepare	*To Facilitate*
■ Identify learning points.	■ Follow the format (you ask leading questions, learners respond, you follow up).
■ Develop leading questions for each learning point.	■ Be flexible and follow learners' interests.
■ Prepare for anticipated responses.	■ End the discussion by summarizing major learning points.
■ Prepare remarks to supplement learners' responses.	■ Make transition to next content.
■ Build transitions to next learning point.	■ Develop leading questions for each learning point.

Modeling/demonstration: Use to help learners acquire a skill or behavior.

To Prepare	*To Facilitate*
■ Identify steps in the process.	■ Tell learners the process/behavior.
■ Determine how to demonstrate the skills/behavior.	■ Demonstrate the skills/behavior.
■ Determine how the learners will practice the skills/behavior.	■ Answer learners' questions.
■ Determine how feedback will be given.	■ Set up the practice exercise.
■ Determine instrument(s) to assess the quality of performance.	■ Facilitate the practice exercise.
■ Develop debrief questions.	■ Provide for facilitator and peer feedback.
	■ Conduct debrief.

Case study: Use to help learners analyze problems and provide a solution.

To Prepare	*To Facilitate*
■ Identify learning points.	■ Give the learners the case.
■ Determine if work is to be individual or team.	■ Give instructions: 　1. format for response 　2. groupings 　3. time 　4. questions.
■ Develop case contents: characters, issues, context, questions, response format/structure, learning solution(s).	■ Provide break-out rooms or team tables.
■ Develop debrief questions and responses.	■ Allow learners to work on the case.
	■ Provide for facilitator and peer feedback.
	■ Conduct debrief.

Role play: Use to train for interpersonal skills.

To Prepare	*To Facilitate*
■ Identify learning points.	■ Present the role play situation.
■ Develop the scenario, including situation, roles for learners and role descriptions, and script.	■ Set up the role play: 　1. groupings 　2. time 　3. materials 　4. questions to consider.
■ Provide instructions.	■ Have learners enact the role play.
■ Develop debrief questions.	■ Provide for facilitator and peer feedback.
	■ Conduct debrief.

Facilitation/Presentation Skills Checklist

The following checklist can be used as a job aid to support the development of your facilitation and presentation skills.

- ☐ Use appropriate verbal and nonverbal communication techniques.
- ☐ Use voice (tone, projection, inflection), gestures, and eye contact.
- ☐ Use examples, personal experiences, stories, and/or humor.
- ☐ Use various questioning techniques.
- ☐ Paraphrase/restate participants' questions, comments, and observations.
- ☐ Promote participant discussion and involvement.
- ☐ Provide complete and timely feedback to participants.
- ☐ Provide time for participants to ask questions and/or raise concerns.
- ☐ Implement a variety of instructional/learning strategies (such as guided discussions, case studies, role plays, small group work with feedback, and assessments).
- ☐ Plan and facilitate debriefs so learning is processed.
- ☐ Adjust activities, time, pace, content, and sequencing to accommodate specific learner needs.
- ☐ Apply media (such as video, overheads, computer projection, wallboards, props, and flipcharts).
- ☐ Involve participants in establishing and maintaining the learning environment.
- ☐ Use warm-up activities to gain participant involvement.
- ☐ Manage group interaction, involve quiet participants, and manage participants who try to monopolize the interaction.
- ☐ Reinforce content as participants answer each others' questions.

Media Decision Table

The following media decision table is a helpful summary for evaluating characteristics and effective use of various media choices.

1. Obtain information from the participants.

Method	*Choice of Media*
■ Discussion	■ Blank flipchart ■ Blank transparency ■ Blackboard or whiteboard
■ Subgroups or teams	■ Prepared assignment presented by: 1. Blackboard or whiteboard 2. Flipcharts 3. Transparencies 4. Handouts
■ Testing	■ Handouts ■ Behavioral checklists

2. Present information to the participants.

Method	*Choice of Media*
■ Presentation	■ Prepared flipcharts ■ Video recordings ■ Transparencies ■ Handouts ■ 35 mm slides ■ Computer projection
■ General discussion	■ Prepared flipcharts ■ Transparencies ■ Handouts ■ 35 mm slides
■ Modeling	■ Prerecorded videotapes ■ Prerecorded audio tapes ■ Trainer acting as a model
■ Brainstorming	■ Blank flipcharts

3. Participants process the information.

Method	Choice of Media
■ General discussion	■ Prepared flipcharts ■ Transparencies ■ Handouts
■ Subgroups or teams	■ Blank flipcharts ■ Handouts
■ Case studies	■ Handouts ■ Computer
■ Games	■ Handouts
■ Simulation	■ Handouts ■ Computer

4. Participants utilize the information.

Method	Choice of Media
■ Role play	■ Video recording equipment ■ Worksheet handouts ■ Audio recording equipment
■ Games	■ Handouts
■ Simulations and case studies	■ Handouts ■ Computer

These last activities give you an indication of whether the participants have understood the points you want to emphasize and enable you to begin evaluating their learning. Using these methods and media is probably different from any teaching or training you have done or anticipated doing. You'll find you'll enjoy both the challenge and the final product!

Hints for Presentations

Educational presentations place the emphasis on learning. The facilitator and participants are actually partners in the learning process. Here are some hints:

- Be natural—be yourself. Minimize any distracting behaviors or habits.
- Stay in contact with the participants, and work to eliminate any known barriers.
- Avoid presenting too much information; 15 to 20 minutes of straight presentation is about the maximum that participants can tolerate.
- Pay attention to how participants are reacting.
- Establish pace and tone that is comfortable for you; check if the participants are OK with it.
- Maintain eye contact with participants in all areas of the room.
- Once a point has been adequately covered, summarize it and move on. Restate essential points frequently to reinforce the continuity of your presentation.
- Use pauses to let an important point sink in or to encourage participant reaction.
- Avoid clichés and jargon.
- Don't make excuses for content missing from your session; they call unnecessary attention to imperfections.

Hints for Using Visual Aids
Overhead transparencies
- Look at the screen for positioning, then at participants.
- Place the transparency on the glass before turning on the switch.

- Point to items on the transparency, not on the screen.
- If you don't have a pointer, you can use a sharp pencil.
- Keep transparencies in order, and be ready to place the next one on the glass.
- Place your own transparencies on the glass; avoid asking others to do it for you.
- Occasionally, move away from the projector to interact with participants.
- Try to follow the "6 X 6 rule": six lines, each with no more than six words.
- All text should be at least 18 point; larger if there are more than 30 participants.
- Be careful about using an enlarged copy of a cartoon or comic strip because of the detail of the pictures or the amount of writing.
- If you use frames or sleeves for the overhead transparencies, write your notes on the edges, and talk from those.
- Do not use red as one of the marker colors. It looks different under fluorescent lights and may have a psychological connotation of "stop," subconsciously affecting the readers' perception of the written message.

Flipcharts

- Write large enough for participants to read the information.
- Write clearly and neatly.
- Avoid too much information; capture key ideas.
- As you list items, use more than one color of marker, and alternate the colors by item.
- Flipcharts can be prepared in advance and covered with acetate. This will allow reuse.

35 mm slides

■ Avoid turning the lights down too low; it hinders communication and note taking.

■ Use a remote control, and avoid pointing it at the projector as if it's a gun.

■ Check to make certain that the slides are in order and arranged right side up.

■ Avoid reading from the screen; look at the participants, and talk to them.

■ Move around; maintain contact with the participants.

PowerPoint presentations (as LCD panels)

■ PowerPoint presentations add visual quality, use of animation, and ease of use.

■ Be familiar with the slide organizer, since going back to previous slides can be difficult.

■ Have a set of overheads as backup.

■ Use a remote so your movements are not limited.

Videos

If you buy a video, do not feel that you have to show it in its entirety. Videos can be very effective if you use only short segments of 30 seconds to a few minutes. You want to reinforce your content, so do not waste a lot of time with the entire video.

General

Be sensitive to copyright restrictions on materials you want to use. Check with the author or with the permissions department of the publisher.

5 CONCLUDING REMARKS

Congratulations! You have now completed the workbook. You have learned to design and develop a short training program incorporating adult learning principles and design and development skills. Using various instructional strategies, you have incorporated skill, practice, and application into your program. Having designed and developed a course based on identified needs, you now have knowledge of some facilitation practices to enhance your delivery. All of this makes for a more meaningful learning experience for the learners and increases the probability that the new knowledge and skills will be used on the job for positive change.

By becoming more skilled in design, development, and facilitation, you are improving your contribution to enhancing the intellectual capital of your organization and its competitiveness in the marketplace. But do not stop here. Continue your work in human resource development through continued study and by supporting other training initiatives that can use your content knowledge and your design, development, and facilitation skills. Good luck in your future endeavors!

APPENDIX: A

Example for Design, Development, and Delivery of a Learning Experience

This example of a course on the learning organization provides illustrations of the content areas presented in the course, *Making Learning Work*. The format used to present the example is the job aid for course design, development, and delivery. A blank job aid is provided on page 77 for your ongoing course development efforts. After each heading, a page number indicates where content related to that subject can be found in this guide.

Phase I: Design

☑ **Align With Needs Analysis:** State the identified needs for the course you are designing. (Refer to page 10.)

Needs analysis was conducted through questionnaires, telephone interviews, and focus groups. The results of the analysis indicated the need for the company to foster an environment of learning, while capturing intellectual capital. This should result in continuous improvement of corporate performance, competitive positioning, and customer satisfaction.

☑ **Determine Class: Audience Profile, Mix, and Size:** Profile your audience. (Refer to pages 11–12.)

The audience for this course will be professionals within business units. Ideally, their manager will have gone through a similar course designed for the management group.

☑ **Develop Course Overview, Theme, and Goals:** Briefly state the aspects of your area of expertise that you want to share with your audience, and describe the results you would like for your audience to gain from your information. (Refer to pages 12–13.)

Area of expertise
I have been involved in a task force looking at developing an environment that supports learning in our organization. Additionally, I have done research on the subject and have been implementing some of the concepts in my business unit. Due to this, I am gaining a reputation as a champion of sharing intellectual capital through the concepts of a learning organization.

Results
I want this organization to view learning as a way to gain and share intellectual capital, resulting in a more competitive organization. To do this, we must understand what a learning organization is, identify the drivers of our becoming a learning organization, and implement various techniques to develop and support a learning environment. The ultimate results will be continuous improvement of our processes, products, and services; improved competitive positioning; and increased customer satisfaction.

Write your course theme and goals. (Refer to page 13.)

Theme
Create and sustain a learning environment that supports continuous learning and retaining/sharing intellectual capital.

Goals
■ Develop a common mindset concerning what a learning organization is and its importance to the company.

- *Develop and sustain an environment supportive of individual, team, and organizational learning.*
- *Develop and sustain systems and processes to capture, retain, and share intellectual capital. Align the recognition and reward systems with this effort.*

☑ **Identify Instructional Strategies:** Write your content outline and initial instructional strategies. Use additional paper as needed. (Refer to pages 14–15.)

Content Outline	*Instructional Strategies*
■ *Introduction*	■ *Facilitated discussion, small group work and report back based on actual scenarios*
■ *Drivers for a Learning Organization*	■ *Facilitated discussion, small group work and report back on unit examples*
■ *Defining the Learning Organization*	■ *Presentation*
■ *How Organizational Learning Takes Place*	■ *Presentation, facilitated discussion, small group work and report back, peer teaching, film clips followed by facilitated discussion after each clip*
■ *Techniques for Becoming a Learning Organization*	■ *Facilitated discussion, small group work and report back on requirements, peer teaching*
■ *Individual Leadership Skills*	■ *Small group work and report back, peer teaching*
■ *Implementing the Concepts*	■ *Small group work for force field analysis and action planning, peer coaching*

☑ **Identify SMEs and Customers for Design Review:** Indicate the people who need to review the design. (Refer to page 15.)
- *The three program sponsors*
- *Six selected managers / directors who participated in the managerial program development and delivery*

☑ **Determine Prerequisites:** Identify prerequisites for the course you are designing. (Refer to page 16.)
> *Reading of preread articles and preparation to peer teach*

☑ **Identify Preferred Delivery Mechanism:** Indicate the delivery mechanism or mechanisms for the course you are designing. (Refer to pages 16–17.)
> *Classroom / facilitation supported by interactive instructional strategies*

☑ **Consider Media:** Indicate your initial media for the course you are designing. (Refer to pages 17–18, 34, and 53–57.)
- *Overheads*
- *Prepared flipcharts and blank flipcharts*
- *Videos*

Phase II: Development

☑ **Establish Learning Objectives:** Write your learning objectives to meet the criteria for each module or unit you defined in your content outline. A module would also include participant introduction, course agenda, participant expectations, programs norms or standard operating procedures, facilitator introduction, theme and goals, and so forth. Use additional paper if required. (Refer to pages 26–30.)

Module 1: As a result of this program, participants will be able to

- *identify five drivers to a learning organization*
- *describe the three learning organization techniques*
- *list three learning organization individual leadership skills*
- *using forms provided, identify four drivers and four restraining forces applicable to moving toward a learning organization; develop and implement strategies to implement such a movement*
- *using the forms provided, develop six individual tactics that will support the drivers or reduce/eliminate the restraining forces identified above.*

☑ **Develop/Write the Content and Link to Learning Objectives:** Indicate the course or module benefits to the participants, the link to prior and subsequent modules or courses, the link to the needs assessment, and describe your warm-up exercise. (Refer to pages 30–32.) Because of the length of this program, excerpts will be used. The bold-faced words in parentheses refer to a design and development attribute.

Introduction

Introduce the course through examples of other organizations that have implemented learning organization concepts and the performance benefits that they have derived from using these concepts. Indicate that the only sustainable competitive advantage is the knowledge worker. By capturing and sharing this knowledge, the company can continuously improve its operations and add value to the customer **(benefits, importance, and link to needs assessment).**

Each of the four teams is given a different actual scenario experienced by this or another company. They are asked to define the issue, determine the implications of this scenario, and indicate its relationship to the concepts of being a learning organization. (They have preread materials that provide the needed information to respond to this exercise.) After the teams report back, summarize with a large group discussion (**warm-up**).

In this workshop, we will look at how your organization (business function/unit) can move toward becoming a learning organization. We will address your understanding of what a learning organization is and how you can promote a learning environment in your sphere of influence. The output will be strategies and tactics to be implemented on the job in a selected area of individual, team, or organizational learning (**preview**).

Also, we have developed the following learning objectives (see above) and the following agenda, which becomes the program map (**preview**). Facilitator would present the agenda.

Body: theory and skill development

(This content will cover the techniques of learning organizations.)

We have just completed our discussion on the different types of learning and individual learning (**link back to content**). Now we want to discuss some of the techniques of learning organizations (**preview**). These techniques come from Garvin's article, "Building a Learning Organization," which you read as part of your preread material (**link back to preread material**). Would the team responsible for teaching the major concepts of that article share with us Garvin's techniques and apply those concepts to your business function (**instructional strategy: peer teaching**)?

Some of the major points to look for include the following:

Learning from the past: Companies must review successes and failures, assess them systematically, and record the lessons in a form that employees find open and accessible. Organizational memory requires that the relevant information is stored and can be retrieved.

This provides a history of what has or has not worked, enabling companies to replicate successes and prevent a repeat of mistakes. A productive failure is one that leads to insights, understanding, and therefore adds to corporate wisdom (**facilitator note**).

Learning from others: Sources include benchmarking, input from customer, suppliers, competitors, and so forth. The environment must be receptive. Managers must be open and nondefensive. The culture must accept criticism.

Transfer to others: For learning to be more than local, knowledge must spread quickly and efficiently throughout the organization. Mechanisms include various kinds of reports, tours and site visits, job rotations, and education and training programs.

Divide the group into three subgroups, one for each practice. Each group is to apply a concept to their function (**instructional strategy**).

For learning from the past, ask, "For your function to do this, what is required?" Have participants reference the Garvin article. Suggested responses include the following:

- technology to store and retrieve learnings
- an environment conducive to sharing success and failures
- incentives to share learnings and a way to determine the value of the contribution
- a way to determine what information is to be included, develop a criteria
- a consistent methodology to capture learnings in context.

For learning from others, ask, "For your function to do this, what is required?" Suggested responses include the following:

- create an environment open to criticism
- identify specific sources (What criteria will you use to select those sources?)
- develop mechanisms to capture and share the information
- identify what resources are required.

For transfer to others, ask, "For your function to do this, what is required?" Characterize the environment of a learning organization. Suggested responses include the following:

- identify the mechanisms (video conference, reports, job transfer/-sharing, internal publications, forums, and training programs)
- incentives for persons to share
- criteria and format for sharing valuable information in context
- a culture and environment that encourages transfer and use of knowledge (an environment that allows the testing of assumptions; the practice of ideas; differing perspectives; lateral communication; provides strong networks; allows for critical examination of processes, method, and values; allows for the redefinition of roles; and is nonthreatening) **(satisfies the third learning objective)**.

Summary

Through Garvin's article and our various activities, we have been able to understand and apply the techniques of a learning organization, including learning from the past, learning from others, and transfer to others. We have seen how part of the requirement is a technology that enables the implementation of these techniques. We have also seen how we must create an environment that supports these techniques. Some of the factors you indicated include an openness to criticism, a recognition and reward system that supports these techniques, seeing failures as opportunities to learn, developing criteria to determine what information should be retained and in what format for learning, and a methodology to capture learnings in context. While not all inclusive of our insights, these summarize some of the requirements to implement these learning organization techniques successfully **(summary)**.

To implement these techniques requires leadership skills. We are not talking about a position, but individual leadership skills. In the next section, we will discuss several individual leadership skills that will help you create a learning organization **(preview)**.

☑ **Conduct Content Review:** Indicate whom you will invite to the content review. Some of these participants include those who participated in the design review. (Refer to pages 32–33.)

■ *The three program sponsors*
■ *The six selected managers / directors who participated in the managerial program development and delivery*
■ *Six to eight professionals representing the four different business functions / units*

☑ **Determine and Develop Instructional Strategies:** Having developed the course content, determine the instructional strategies you will use for each module. The instructional strategies should relate to and support your module learning objectives and course content. (Refer to pages 33–34.)

Module 1 (introduction):
■ *small group work and report back*

Module 2:
■ *facilitated discussion*
■ *small group work and report back*
■ *peer teaching*

On separate paper, develop your instructional strategies. Include directions and supporting participant material.

Module 1:
■ *small group work and report back:*
   Each of the four teams is given a different actual scenario experienced by their company or another company. They are asked to define the issue, determine the implications of this scenario, and indicate its relationship to the concepts of being a learning organization.

Module 2:

■ *facilitated discussion:*

See the body: theory and skill development portion of the Develop/-Write the Content and Link to Learning Objectives section above.

■ *small group work and report back:*

Divide the group into three subgroups, one for each practice/technique. Each group is to apply the concept to their function and prepare to report back and discuss their ideas. (Facilitator's suggested debrief comments are in the content section above.)

■ *peer teaching:*

The team responsible for teaching the major concepts of the Garvin article is to share Garvin's techniques and apply those concepts to their business function. (Facilitator's suggested debrief comments are in the content section above.)

☑ **Develop/Secure Media:** Develop/secure the actual media to be used in the course delivery. (Refer to pages 17–18, 34–35, and 53–57.)

The media used includes overheads, prepared flipcharts, and videos (some purchased and some internally developed).

☑ **Determine Classroom Layout:** Work with your training department to determine the classroom layout that best meets your program requirements. (Refer to pages 35–36 for suggestions about layouts.)

Since the course is designed to reinforce team interaction and discussion, the layout is for team tables.

☑ **Develop the Instructor/Facilitator Guide:** On separate paper, develop the instructor/facilitator guide for the course. (Refer to page 35.)

An instructor/facilitator guide indicates all topics and subtopics, time-frames, all media, instructional strategies with instructions and responses, and page references to the participants' guide and strategy booklet.

☑ **Develop/Secure Participant Materials:** (Refer to page 37.)
  ☑ Preread material developed/secured:
    ■ *Articles were selected and secured, with reprint permissions.*
    ■ *Schedule for mailings was developed.*
  ☑ Instruction or worksheets developed/secured:
    ■ *Small group work instructions were developed.*
    ■ *Worksheets and prepared flipcharts for the force field analysis and action were developed.*
  ☑ Participant manual developed/secured:
    ■ *Participant manual has been completed with masters ready for duplication.*

☑ **Develop Evaluation Instruments:** Use the course evaluation instrument provided to assess participant reaction. Work with your training department for additional evaluation instruments and an evaluation strategy. (Refer to pages 20–24 and 37.)
  ■ *A pilot evaluation instrument was developed.*
  ■ *A reaction or level 1 instrument was developed.*
  ■ *An instrument to measure if learning took place was developed.*
  ■ *An instrument and process for on-the-job follow-up was developed.*

☑ **Conduct a Pilot Course:** (Refer to pages 37–38.)
  Delivered the course to a selected audience of 16 professionals. Using a specially designed evaluation instrument and verbal feedback, the course was revised and made ready for rollout.

Phase III: Delivery

☑ **Select Qualified Instructor/Facilitator:** Indicate the person or persons selected to lead the course and a summary of their qualifications. (Refer to pages 38–40.)

Name	Qualifications
Jane Doe I	BBA, MBA, Ed.D., 17 years of training experience, well read in learning organizations, eight years of corporate experience
Jane Doe II	BA, MA, seven years of corporate experience, five years in two of the business functions, two years of training experience

☑ **Conduct Train-the-Trainer:** Conduct a train-the-trainer session to ensure that the selected leader both understands and can present the content and instructional strategies. (Refer to pages 41–42.)

A one-day session was provided to selected facilitators. During the session, content was presented, integrating instructional strategies and use of media. Facilitators had the opportunity to practice delivering and facilitating sections of the course. Facilitators were provided a copy of the leader's guide prior to the session for their preparation.

☑ **Roll Out Course:** With the assistance of the training department, make necessary arrangements for making the course available to your target audience. (Refer to pages 41–42.)

Regional delivery, preferably in corporate facilities, offered once per month. A complete list of requirements was provided to the facility, including transportation and lodging for those participants traveling.

APPENDIX: B

Checklist for Design, Development, and Delivery of a Learning Experience

This checklist is designed as a quick reference and structure for your design, development, and delivery efforts. Check the appropriate box when you complete each step. For content around each step, refer to the corresponding section in the guide.

Phase I: Design

- [ ] Secure needs analysis data
- [ ] Consider cultural adaptability
- [ ] Identify target audience
    - [ ] Understand audience profile
    - [ ] Determine class mix
    - [ ] Determine class size
- [ ] Align course content to needs analysis
- [ ] Develop course theme
- [ ] Develop course goals
- [ ] Develop high-level outline
- [ ] Consider flow/format for the modules
- [ ] Identify initial instructional strategies
- [ ] Identify SMEs and customers for design review
- [ ] Determine prerequisites
- [ ] Identify preferred delivery mechanism
- [ ] Consider media
- [ ] Consider evaluation

Phase II: Development

- [ ] Establish learning objectives
  - [ ] Determine that they are measurable
  - [ ] Determine that they contain the performance, conditions, and criteria components
- [ ] Develop content and write materials
  - [ ] Determine that content links to and supports learning objectives
  - [ ] Conduct content review
  - [ ] Invite appropriate participants
  - [ ] Make revisions
  - [ ] Develop instructional strategies
    - [ ] Determine that instructional strategies support the content and learning objectives
  - [ ] Develop/secure the media
    - [ ] Determine that the media supports the content and enhances learning
- [ ] Determine classroom layout to support the design and instructional strategies
- [ ] Develop instructor/facilitator guide
- [ ] Develop/secure participant materials
  - [ ] Develop participant manual
  - [ ] Develop/secure preread materials
  - [ ] Develop instruments for action planning
  - [ ] Develop required instruction pages and worksheets
- [ ] Develop evaluation instruments
- [ ] Conduct a course pilot
  - [ ] Invite appropriate participants
  - [ ] Make revisions

Phase III: Delivery

☐ Select qualified instructor/facilitator
 ☐ Determine that the instructor is knowledgeable of the company, business function/unit, and subject matter
 ☐ Determine that the instructor is experienced in facilitation
 ☐ Determine that the instructor is credible with the target audience
 ☐ Determine that the instructor has compatible values
☐ Conduct train-the-trainer
 ☐ Prepare materials
 ☐ Prepare media
 ☐ Complete administrative/logistical support
☐ Roll out course
 ☐ Secure support from your training department

APPENDIX: C

Job Aid for Design, Development, and Delivery of a Learning Experience

This job aid is to assist a designer by providing a concise format to design a course. After each heading, the reference page number provided indicates where content related to that subject can be found in *Creating Training Courses (When You're Not a Trainer)*. Sequence is important since some earlier activities form the basis for later decisions. Check the box beside each item after completing the corresponding step.

Phase I: Design

☐ **Align With Needs Analysis:** State the identified needs for the course you are designing. (Refer to page 10.)

_____

_____

_____

_____

☐ **Determine Class: Audience Profile, Mix, and Size:** Profile your audience. (Refer to pages 11–12).

_____

_____

_____

_____

☐ **Develop Course Overview, Theme, and Goals:** Briefly state the aspects of your area of expertise that you want to share with your audience, and describe the results you would like for your audience to gain from your information. (Refer to pages 12–13.)

Area of expertise

_____

_____

_____

_____

Results

_____

_____

_____

_____

Write your course theme and goals. (Refer to page 13).

Theme

_____

_____

_____

_____

Goals

_____

_____

_____

_____

☐ **Identify Instructional Strategies:** Write your content outline and instructional strategies. Use additional paper as needed. (Refer to page 14.)

Content Outline	*Instructional Strategies*
_____	_____
_____	_____
_____	_____
_____	_____
_____	_____
_____	_____
_____	_____
_____	_____

☐ **Identify SMEs and Customers for Design Review:** Indicate the people who need to review the design. (Refer to page 15.)

_____

_____

_____

_____

☐ **Determine Prerequisites:** Identify prerequisites for the course you are designing. (Refer to page 16).

_____

_____

_____

_____

☐ **Identify Preferred Delivery Mechanism:** Indicate the delivery mechanism or mechanisms for the course you are designing. (Refer to pages 16–17.)

_____

_____

_____

_____

☐ **Consider Media:** Indicate your initial media for the course you are designing. (Refer to pages 17–18, 34–35, and 53–57.)

_____

_____

_____

_____

Phase II: Development

☐ **Establish Learning Objectives:** Write your learning objectives to meet the criteria for each module or unit you defined in your content outline. A module would also include participant introduction, course agenda, participant expectations, programs norms or standard operating procedures, facilitator introduction, theme and goals, and so forth. Use additional paper if required. (Refer to pages 26–30.)

Module 1

_____

_____

_____

_____

Module 2

_____

_____

_____

_____

Module 3

_____

_____

_____

_____

Module 4

_____

_____

_____

_____

☐ **Develop/Write the Content and Link to Learning Objectives:** Indicate the course or module benefits to the participants, the link to prior and subsequent modules or courses, the link to the needs assessment, and describe your warm-up exercise. (Refer to pages 30–32.)

The content can be divided into three areas: the introduction, the body—including the presentation of the underlying theory and skill development—and the summary. On separate paper, develop/write the content for the course.

Benefits:

_____

_____

Link/fit to prior and subsequent modules or courses:

_____

_____

_____

_____

Link to needs assessment:

_____

_____

_____

_____

Describe your warm-up exercise:

_____

_____

_____

_____

☐ **Conduct Content Review:** Indicate whom you will invite to the content review. Some of these participants include those who participated in the design review. (Refer to pages 32–33.)

_____

_____

_____

_____

☐ **Determine and Develop Instructional Strategies:** Having developed the course content, determine the instructional strategies you will use for each module. The instructional strategies should relate to and support your module learning objectives and course content. (Refer to pages 33–34.)

Module 1

_____

_____

_____

_____

Module 2

_____

_____

_____

_____

Module 3

_____

_____

_____

_____

Module 4

_____

_____

_____

_____

On separate paper, fully develop the instructional strategies selected, including directions and any supporting participant material.

Module 1

_____

_____

_____

Module 2

_____

_____

_____

Module 3

_____

_____

_____

Module 4

_____

_____

_____

☐ **Develop/Secure Media:** Develop/secure the actual media to be used in the course delivery. (Refer to pages 17–18, 34–35, and 53–57.)

_____

_____

_____

_____

☐ **Determine Classroom Layout:** Work with your training department to determine the classroom layout that best meets your program requirements. (Refer to pages 35–36 for suggestions about layouts.)

_____

_____

_____

_____

☐ **Develop the Instructor/Facilitator Guide:** On separate paper, develop the instructor/facilitator guide for the course. (Refer to page 35.)

_____

_____

_____

_____

☐ **Develop/Secure Participant Materials:** (Refer to page 37.)

    ☐ Preread material developed/secured: _____

    ☐ Instruction or worksheets developed/secured: _____

    ☐ Participant manual developed/secured: _____

☐ **Develop Evaluation Instruments:** Use the course evaluation instrument provided to assess participant reaction. Work with your training department for additional evaluation instruments and an evaluation strategy. (Refer to pages 20–24 and 37.)

_____

_____

_____

_____

☐ **Conduct a Pilot Course:** (Refer to pages 37–38.)

_____

_____

_____

_____

Phase III: Delivery

☐ **Select Qualified Instructor/Facilitator:** Indicate the person or persons selected to lead the course and a summary of their qualifications. (Refer to pages 38–40.)

Name	*Qualifications*

☐ **Conduct Train-the-Trainer:** Conduct a train-the-trainer session to ensure that the selected leader both understands and can present the content and instructional strategies. (Refer to pages 41–42.)

_____

_____

_____

☐ **Roll Out Course:** With the assistance of the training department, make necessary arrangements for making the course available to your target audience. (Refer to pages 41–42.)

_____

_____

_____

GLOSSARY OF TERMS

Brainstorming: An instructional strategy that promotes the generation of ideas without evaluation or analysis.

Case Study: A written account of a real or fictitious event or situation, including facts and opinions in enough detail for learners to analyze the problem or problems presented and make decisions to solve the problem. Generally, the closer the case depicts reality, the better the organizational learning.

Demonstration/Practice: See modeling.

Design/Development: The process of structuring content, whether it be knowledge, information, theories, concepts, procedures, and so forth; instructional strategies; and media into meaningful learning experiences with the result of enhanced individual performance, business unit performance, or both.

Development: Has no direct relation to a particular job, but helps individuals and organizations cope with a rapidly changing environment. Development might include stretch assignments, courses, experiential learning, or special assignments that keep people learning, broadening their knowledge and experience.

Education: Learning experiences to prepare a person for a different, yet identified, future job. It is related to career planning.

Exercise: A structured learning experience supported by instructions and debrief explanation with application to the job; allows for discovery or application of concepts.

Experience-Centered: The foundation of experience-based training is that people learn best by doing. Some examples include rope courses and outward-bound adventure training. The experiences are structured around perceived risk-taking activities necessitating group and individual challenge. This type of training provides learning experiences that represent organizational situations.

Evaluation: A process of appraising training to determine and improve its value; the determination of the effectiveness of training programs; a measure of the extent to which objectives were met. (Also see Level 1, Level 2, Level 3, and Level 4 Evaluation below.)

Facilitation/Guided Discussion: A planned, two-way discussion where the facilitator draws out learning points from the learners by asking questions. As the learners make the points, the facilitator supplements and applies the learning and transitions to the next learning point. This is used best when learners know something about the content.

Games: Training activities that blend activity, competition, and fun with simulation. Because games are constructed with rules and limited consequences, they provide a safe way to explore training content and test for recall, recognition, and skills.

Instructional Strategies: Activities that determine how learning will take place, including role plays, games, case studies, facilitative discussion, simulations, and so forth.

Learning Objectives: Statements about what the learner should know and be able to do as a result of the training.

Learning Strategies: See instructional strategies.

Lecture: Information as knowledge, theories, and concepts presented in a one-way format by the facilitator; participants ask questions for clarification.

Level 1 Evaluation of Participant Reaction: The process of collecting the subjective perceptions of participants, usually immediately following a learning experience. It is a measure of customer satisfaction in areas such as the degree to which program objectives were met, pace and sequence, quality of media, appropriateness of content, facilitator knowledge and skill, quality of participant materials, quality and variety of media, and the effectiveness of instructional strategies.

Level 2 Evaluation of Learning and Application: The change in knowledge, skills, and attitude as a result of the learning experience. The process of collecting and analyzing information to determine how much the participants learned and can apply the new knowledge and skills (in the learning experience) as a result of the learning experience.

Level 3 Evaluation of Transfer of Learning: The use of knowledge and skills learned in one situation (the learning experience) now applied to another situation (on the job). The process of assessing whether the knowledge, skills, attitude, or all of these taught in the learning experience are being used on the job and to what extent. Includes an assessment of the environment to identify the barriers and enabling forces to transfer.

Level 4 Evaluation of Impact or Business Results: The process of determining how much and how well training led to a change in a business measurement as organizational productivity, customer satisfaction, reduction in time, increased output, and so forth, or the contribution the learning experience made to realizing the organization's business plan. Business impact can be measured by calculating the return on investment (ROI) resulting from the learning experience.

Modeling: The facilitator, or some other leader (as on videotapes), demonstrates a skill or behavior, which is then analyzed and practiced by the learners. The learners then receive feedback on their practice. The desired performance is scripted to provide a good example of the required behavior.

Needs Assessment: Process of identifying the amount, kind, and depth of training needs that must be developed for a target audience. A systematic method of assessing the state of individual and business unit performance and identifying the causal factors of that performance.

Organization Development (OD): Various activities and interventions designed to improve the relationships between people and business units.

Role Play: A structured exercise where learners are given a problem situation and assigned predetermined roles. The learners must reenact the situation and solve the problem situation. To support the role play, observers and observational criteria are established. After the role play, the learners debrief the activity with lessons learned and suggestions for improved performance. Role plays help learners learn interpersonal skills.

Simulation: A culminating activity that replicates reality and requires the learner to use what has been taught. Simulations are intended to provide opportunities to interact with realistic representations of reality.

Subject Matter Expert (SME): A person perceived to have significant expertise and organizational credibility in a particular subject matter, independent of organizational position.

Training: Learning that is directly related to the person's current job. Training is required on the basis of a need for improved current job performance.

BIBLIOGRAPHY

Chalosfsky, Neal E., and Carlene Reinhart. *Effective Human Resource Development.* San Francisco: Jossey-Bass Publishers, 1988.

Charles, C. Leslie, and Chris Clarke-Epstein. *The Instant Trainer: Quick Tips on How to Teach Others What You Know.* New York: The McGraw-Hill Companies, 1997.

Clark, Ruth Ann. *Developing Technical Training.* New York: Addison-Wesley Publishing Company, 1989.

Craig, Robert, editor. *The ASTD Training & Development Handbook: A Guide to Human Resource Development.* (4th edition) New York: The McGraw-Hill Companies, 1996.

Craig, Robert. *Training and Development Handbook.* New York: The McGraw-Hill Companies, 1987.

Davis, James R., and Adelaide B. Davis. *Effective Training Strategies: A Comprehensive Guide to Maximizing Learning in Organizations.* San Francisco: Berrett-Koehler Publishers, 1998.

Eitington, Julius E. *The Winning Trainer: Winning Ways to Involve People in Learning.* Houston: Gulf Publishing Company, 1996.

Frank, Darlene. *Terrific Training Materials: High Impact Graphic Designs for Workbooks, Handouts, Instructor Guides, and Job Aids.* Amherst, Massachusetts: Human Resources Development Press, 1996.

Gagne, Robert, Leslie Briggs, and Walter Wager. *Principles of Instructional Design*. San Francisco: Holt, Rinehart, and Winston, 1988.

Gupta, Kavita. *A Practical Guide to Needs Assessment*. San Francisco: Jossey-Bass Publishers, 1998.

Hart, L.B. *Saying Hello: Getting Your Group Started*. King of Prussia, Pennsylvania: Organization Design and Development, 1989.

Kirkpatrick, Donald. *Evaluating Training Programs: The Four Levels*. San Francisco: Berrett-Koehler Publishers, 1994.

Knowles, Malcolm. *Designs for Adult Learning: Practical Resources, Exercises, and Course Outlines from the Father of Adult Learning*. Alexandria, Virginia: The American Society for Training & Development, 1995.

Knowles, Malcolm. *The Adult Learner: A Neglected Species*. Houston: Gulf Publishing Company, 1984.

Jones, John, and William Bearley. *Energizers for Training and Conferences*. King of Prussia, Pennsylvania: Organization Design and Development, 1989.

Jones, Philip. *Adult Learning in Your Classroom*. Minneapolis: Lakewood Publications, 1982.

Mager, Robert F. *Preparing Instructional Objectives*. Belmont, California: David S. Lake Publishers, 1984.

Mager, Robert F., and Peter Pipe. *Analyzing Performance Problems*. Belmont, California: David S. Lake Publishers, 1984.

Malouf, Doug. *How to Create and Deliver a Dynamic Presentation*. Alexandria, Virginia: The American Society for Training & Development, 1993.

McArdle, Geri E. *Training Design and Delivery: A Single-Source Guide for Every Trainer, Training Manager, and Occasional Trainer.* Alexandria, Virginia: The American Society for Training & Development, 1999.

Milano, Michael, and Diane Ullius. *Designing Powerful Training: The Sequential Iterative Model (SIM).* San Francisco: Jossey-Bass Publishers, 1998.

Mitchell, Garry. *The Trainer's Handbook: The AMA Guide to Effective Training.* New York: American Management Association International, 1998.

Overfield, Karen. *Developing and Managing Organizational Learning: A Guide to Effective Training Project Management.* Alexandria, Virginia: The American Society for Training & Development, 1998.

Pfeiffer, J.W., and J.E. Jones. *Annual Handbook for Group Facilitators.* San Diego: University Associates, 1972-1998.

Pfeiffer, J.W., and J.E Jones. *A Handbook of Structured Experiences for Human Relations Training*, 8 vols. San Diego: University Associates, 1972-1998.

Rylatt, Alastair, and Kevin Lohan. *Creating Training Miracles.* San Francisco: Jossey-Bass Publishers, 1997.

Silberman, Mel. *Active Training: A Handbook of Techniques, Designs, Case Examples, and Tips.* (2d edition) San Francisco: Jossey-Bass Publishers, 1998.

Thorne, Kaye, and Alex Machray *Training on a Shoestring: Getting the Most from Your Time, Your Budgets, and Your Staff.* London: Kogan Page Limited; Sterling, Virginia: Stylus Publishing, 1998.

ABOUT THE AUTHOR

Donald V. McCain is founder and principal of Performance Advantage Group, an organization dedicated to helping companies gain competitive advantage through the development of their human resources. To meet the needs of his customers, he formed a subsidiary organization, the Customer Value Institute, which focuses on telecom and information technology companies.

Prior to forming his own companies, McCain was a single contributor and manager of marketing and sales education and leadership development for Nortel, a $13 billion global telecommunications company. As part of the NT Learning Institute, he designed and implemented learning experiences in management, leadership, and functional areas including marketing and sales. In addition to telecommunications, he worked in human resource development (HRD) and salary administration for a $200 million publishing organization.

McCain has provided design/development, evaluation, and certification consultation and projects for companies such as Lucent Technologies, Nortel, Hewitt Associates, GlaxoWellcome, Bell Atlantic, American Axle, ACT, and TCS Management Group. He continues to consult and write on various aspects of HRD. Currently, he provides design/development and delivery work with American Management Association in its HRD curriculum.

McCain has been in the field of HRD for more than 21 years specializing in the design, development, delivery, and evaluation of learning experiences, and processes and strategies for transfer and return-on-investment. He holds a bachelor of business administration in marketing and economics, a master of divinity, a master of business administration in human resources and marketing, and a doctorate of education in HRD from Vanderbilt University.